Lessons on Demand Pr[ess]

# Study Guide
# Student Workbook for Brown Girl Dreaming

By:

John Pennington

The lessons on demand series is designed to provide ready to use resources for novel study. In this book you will find key vocabulary, student organizer pages, and assessments. This guide is the Student Workbook. The Teachers Guide will have answers and an open layout of the activities. The Student Workbook can be used alone but it will not include answers.

Look for bound print <u>Teacher Editions</u> on Amazon.com

PDF versions can be found on Teacherspayteachers.com

NAME:  TEACHER:  Date:

## Vocabulary Box

**Emancipated**

Definition:

Draw:

Related words:

Use in a sentence:

**Revolution**

Definition:

Draw:

Related words:

Use in a sentence:

NAME:

TEACHER:

Date:

## Vocabulary Box

Definition:

Draw:

**Parlor**

Related words:

Use in a sentence:

Definition:

Draw:

**Bouquet**

Related words:

Use in a sentence:

NAME:

TEACHER:

Date:

## Vocabulary Box

Definition:

Draw:

### Scholarship

Related words:

Use in a sentence:

Definition:

Draw:

### Memory

Related words:

Use in a sentence:

NAME:

TEACHER:

Date:

## Vocabulary Box

Definition:

Draw:

**Celebration**

Related words:

Use in a sentence:

Definition:

Draw:

Related words:

Use in a sentence:

NAME:

TEACHER:

Date:

# Quiz

**Question:** Where do they travel to once leaving Ohio?

Answer:

**Question:** What did Jaqueline's father want her name to be?

Answer:

# Question: Who was Odella named after?

Answer:

**Question:** Which set of grandparents do the child spend the most time with?

Answer:

NAME:

TEACHER:

Date:

Assignment:

NAME:

TEACHER:

Date:

## Character Sketch

### Name

### Draw a picture

### Personality/ Distinguishing marks

### Connections to other characters

### Important Actions

NAME:

TEACHER:

Date:

## Character Sketch

Name

Personality/ Distinguishing marks

Draw a picture

Connections to other characters

Important Actions

NAME:

TEACHER:

Date:

Research connections

# What am I researching?

Source (URL, Book, Magazine, Interview)

Facts I found that could be useful or notes

1.

2.

3.

4.

5.

6.

NAME:

TEACHER:

Date:

Research connections

## What am I researching?

Source (URL, Book, Magazine, Interview)

Facts I found that could be useful or notes

1.

2.

3.

4.

5.

6.

NAME:

TEACHER:

Date:

Research connections

## What am I researching?

Source (URL, Book, Magazine, Interview)

Facts I found that could be useful or notes

1.

2.

3.

4.

5.

6.

NAME:

TEACHER:

Date:

Research connections

# What am I researching?

Source (URL, Book, Magazine, Interview)

Facts I found that could be useful or notes

1.

2.

3.

4.

5.

6.

NAME:

TEACHER:

Date:

Research connections

## What am I researching?

Source (URL, Book, Magazine, Interview)

Facts I found that could be useful or notes

1.

2.

3.

4.

5.

6.

NAME:

TEACHER:

Date:

Research connections

# What am I researching?

Source (URL, Book, Magazine, Interview)

Facts I found that could be useful or notes

1.

2.

3.

4.

5.

6.

NAME:

TEACHER:

Date:

# Compare and Contrast Venn Diagram

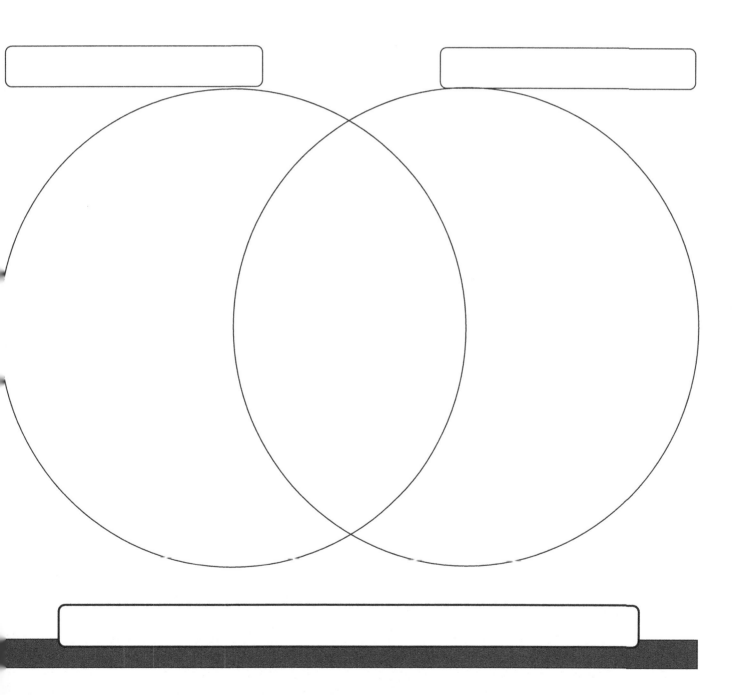

NAME:

TEACHER:

Date:

Draw the Scene: What five things have you included in the scene?

1                              2                              3

4                              5

NAME:

TEACHER:

Date:

Who, What, When, Where, and How

Who

What

Where

When

How

NAME:
TEACHER:
Date:

## Vocabulary Box

Definition:

Draw:

**Slavery**

Related words:

Use in a sentence:

Definition:

Draw:

**Amid**

Related words:

Use in a sentence:

NAME:

TEACHER:

Date:

## Vocabulary Box

Definition:

Draw:

## Subservient

Related words:

Use in a sentence:

Definition:

Draw:

## Inherited

Related words:

Use in a sentence:

NAME:

TEACHER:

Date:

## Vocabulary Box

Definition:

Draw:

**Seamstress**

Related words:

Use in a sentence:

Definition:

Draw:

**Transformed**

Related words:

Use in a sentence:

NAME:

TEACHER:

Date:

## Vocabulary Box

Definition:

Draw:

**Segregated**

Related words:

Use in a sentence:

Definition:

Draw:

**Paradise**

Related words:

Use in a sentence:

NAME:  TEACHER:  Date:

## Vocabulary Box

**Definition:**

**Draw:**

# Superstition

**Related words:**

**Use in a sentence:**

**Definition:**

**Draw:**

# Armageddon

**Related words:**

**Use in a sentence:**

NAME:
TEACHER:
Date:

## Vocabulary Box

**Eternity**

Definition:

Draw:

Related words:

Use in a sentence:

**Infinity**

Definition:

Draw:

Related words:

Use in a sentence:

NAME:

TEACHER:

Date:

# Create the Test

Question: For Mary why would home (Parents home) never be the same?

Answer:

Question: What name does Jacqueline use for her grandfather?

Answer:

Question: When the students had to evacuate Sterling High School, why did they have to attend the elementary school?

Answer:

Question: What religion did the grandmother and children follow?

Answer:

NAME:

TEACHER:

Date:

Assignment:

NAME:

TEACHER:

Date:

## Character Sketch

**Name**

**Personality/ Distinguishing marks**

**Connections to other characters**

**Draw a picture**

**Important Actions**

NAME:

TEACHER:

Date:

## Character Sketch

**Name**

**Draw a picture**

**Personality/ Distinguishing marks**

**Connections to other characters**

**Important Actions**

NAME:

TEACHER:

Date:

## Precognition Sheet

Who ?

What's going to happen?

What will be the result?

Who ?

What's going to happen?

What will be the result?

Who ?

What's going to happen?

What will be the result?

Who ?

What's going to happen?

What will be the result?

How many did you get correct?

NAME:

TEACHER:

Date:

## What would you do?

**Character:** _____

What did they do?

Example from text:

What would you do?

Why would that be better?

**Character:** _____

What did they do?

Example from text:

What would you do?

Why would that be better?

**Character:** _____

What did they do?

Example from text:

What would you do?

Why would that be better?

NAME:

TEACHER:

## Poetry Analysis

Date:

**Name of Poem:**

Subject:
- Text Support:

Plot:
- Text Support:

Theme:
- Text Support:

Setting:
- Text Support:

Tone:
- Text Support:

Important Words and Phrases:

Why are these words and phrases important:

NAME:

TEACHER:

## Poetry Analysis

Date:

**Name of Poem:**

Subject:
- Text Support:

Plot:
- Text Support:

Theme:
- Text Support:

Setting:
- Text Support:

Tone:
- Text Support:

Important Words and Phrases:

Why are these words and phrases important:

NAME:

TEACHER:

## Poetry Analysis

Date:

**Name of Poem:**

Subject:
- Text Support:

Plot:
- Text Support:

Theme:
- Text Support:

Setting:
- Text Support:

Tone:
- Text Support:

Important Words and Phrases:

Why are these words and phrases important:

NAME:

TEACHER:

Date:

## Vocabulary Box

Definition:

Draw:

**Constellation**

Related words:

Use in a sentence:

Definition:

Draw:

**Port**

Related words:

Use in a sentence:

NAME:

TEACHER:

Date:

# Vocabulary Box

Definition:

Draw:

## Composition

Related words:

Use in a sentence:

Definition:

Draw:

## Immature

Related words:

Use in a sentence:

NAME:　　　　　　　　　　TEACHER:

　　　　　　　　　　　　　　Date:

## Vocabulary Box

**Definition:**

**Draw:**

# Temptation

**Related words:**

**Use in a sentence:**

**Definition:**

**Draw:**

# Brilliance

**Related words:**

**Use in a sentence:**

NAME:  
TEACHER:  
Date:

# Vocabulary Box

Definition:

Draw:

## Disappear

Related words:

Use in a sentence:

Definition:

Draw:

## Audience

Related words:

Use in a sentence:

NAME:

TEACHER:

Date:

## Vocabulary Box

Definition:

Draw:

**Resurrection**

Related words:

Use in a sentence:

Definition:

Draw:

**Mecca**

Related words:

Use in a sentence:

NAME:

TEACHER:

Date:

## Vocabulary Box

**Revolution**

- Definition:
- Draw:
- Related words:
- Use in a sentence:

**Feminist**

- Definition:
- Draw:
- Related words:
- Use in a sentence:

NAME:

TEACHER:

Date:

# Create the Test

Question: Why does Roman get sick?

Answer:

Question: What difficulty does Jacqueline have being Odella's younger sister?

Answer:

Question: What skill does Jacqueline realize her has?

Answer:

Question: What happens with daddy Gunnar?

Answer:

NAME:

TEACHER:

Date:

Assignment:

NAME:

TEACHER:

Date:

## Character Sketch

**Name**

**Draw a picture**

**Personality/ Distinguishing marks**

**Connections to other characters**

**Important Actions**

NAME:

TEACHER:

Date:

## Character Sketch

Name

Draw a picture

Personality/ Distinguishing marks

Connections to other characters

Important Actions

NAME:

TEACHER:

Date:

## Character Sketch

**Name**

**Personality/ Distinguishing marks**

**Connections to other characters**

**Draw a picture**

**Important Actions**

NAME:

TEACHER:

Date:

## Character Sketch

**Name**

**Personality/ Distinguishing marks**

**Connections to other characters**

**Draw a picture**

**Important Actions**

NAME:

TEACHER:

Date:

## Character Sketch

### Name

### Personality/ Distinguishing marks

### Draw a picture

### Connections to other characters

### Important Actions

NAME:  TEACHER:  Date:

## Character Sketch

**Name**

**Personality/ Distinguishing marks**

**Draw a picture**

**Connections to other characters**

**Important Actions**

NAME:　　　　　　　　　　　　　TEACHER:

　　　　　　　　　　　　　　　　　　　Date:

## Research connections

# What am I researching?

### Source (URL, Book, Magazine, Interview)

### Facts I found that could be useful or notes

1.

2.

3.

4.

5.

6.

NAME:

TEACHER:

Date:

# Create the Test

Question:

Answer:

Question:

Answer:

Question:

Answer:

Question:

Answer:

NAME:

TEACHER:

Date:

Interview: Who _____

Question:

Answer:

Question:

Answer:

Question:

Answer:

Question:

Answer:

NAME:

TEACHER:

Date:

# Top Ten List

1.
2.
3.
4.
5.
6.
7.
8.
9.
10.

NAME:

TEACHER:

Date:

Write a letter

To:

From:

NAME:

TEACHER:

Date:

Advertisement: Draw an advertisement for _____

NAME:

TEACHER:

Date:

## Chapter to Poem

Assignment: Select 20 words found in the chapter to create a poem where each line is 3 words long.

Title:

_____  _____  _____

_____  _____  _____

_____  _____  _____

_____  _____  _____

_____  _____  _____

NAME:

TEACHER:

Date:

## Character Sketch

**Name**

**Personality/ Distinguishing marks**

**Draw a picture**

**Connections to other characters**

**Important Actions**

NAME:

TEACHER:

Date:

Comic Strip

NAME:

TEACHER:

Date:

# Compare and Contrast Venn Diagram

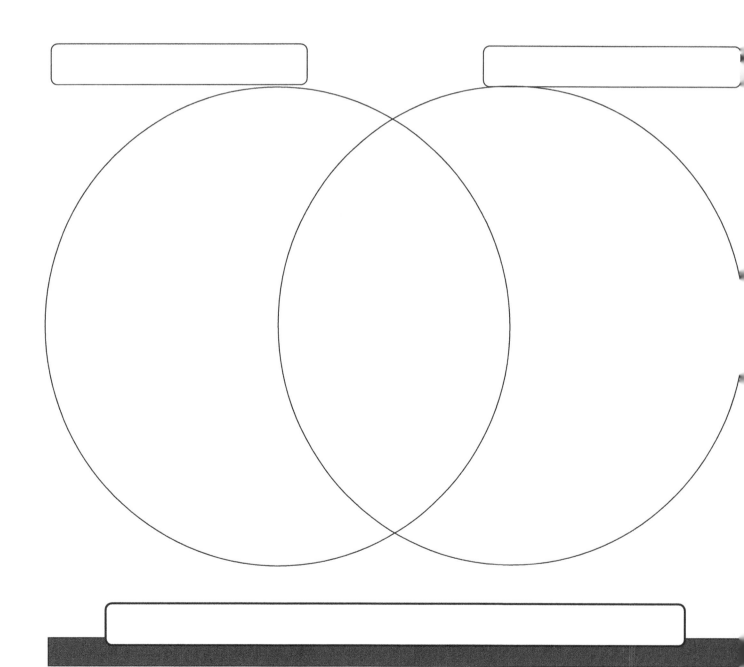

NAME:

TEACHER:

Date:

# Create the Test

Question:

Answer:

Question:

Answer:

Question:

Answer:

Question:

Answer:

NAME:　　　　　　　　　　　　　　　　　TEACHER:

Date:

Draw the Scene: What five things have you included in the scene?

1　　　　　　　　　　　2　　　　　　　　　　　3

4　　　　　　　　　　　5

NAME: _____ TEACHER: _____

Date: _____

Interview: Who _____

Question:

Answer:

Question:

Answer:

Question:

Answer:

Question:

Answer:

NAME:

TEACHER:

Date:

Lost Scene: Write a scene that takes place between _____ and _____

NAME:

TEACHER:

Date:

## Making Connections

What is the connection?

NAME:

TEACHER:

Date:

## Precognition Sheet

| Who ? | What's going to happen? | What will be the result? |

| Who ? | What's going to happen? | What will be the result? |

| Who ? | What's going to happen? | What will be the result? |

| Who ? | What's going to happen? | What will be the result? |

How many did you get correct?

NAME:

TEACHER:

Date:

Assignment: Pyramid

NAME:

TEACHER:

Date:

Research connections

# What am I researching?

Source (URL, Book, Magazine, Interview)

Facts I found that could be useful or notes

1.

2.

3.

4.

5.

6.

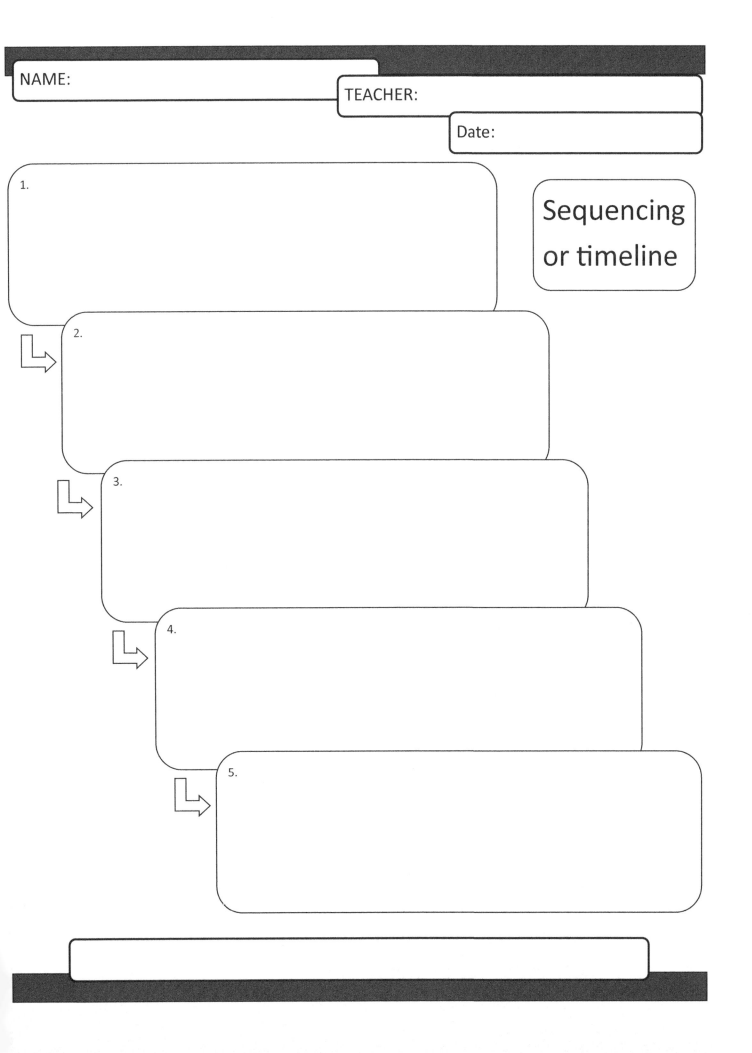

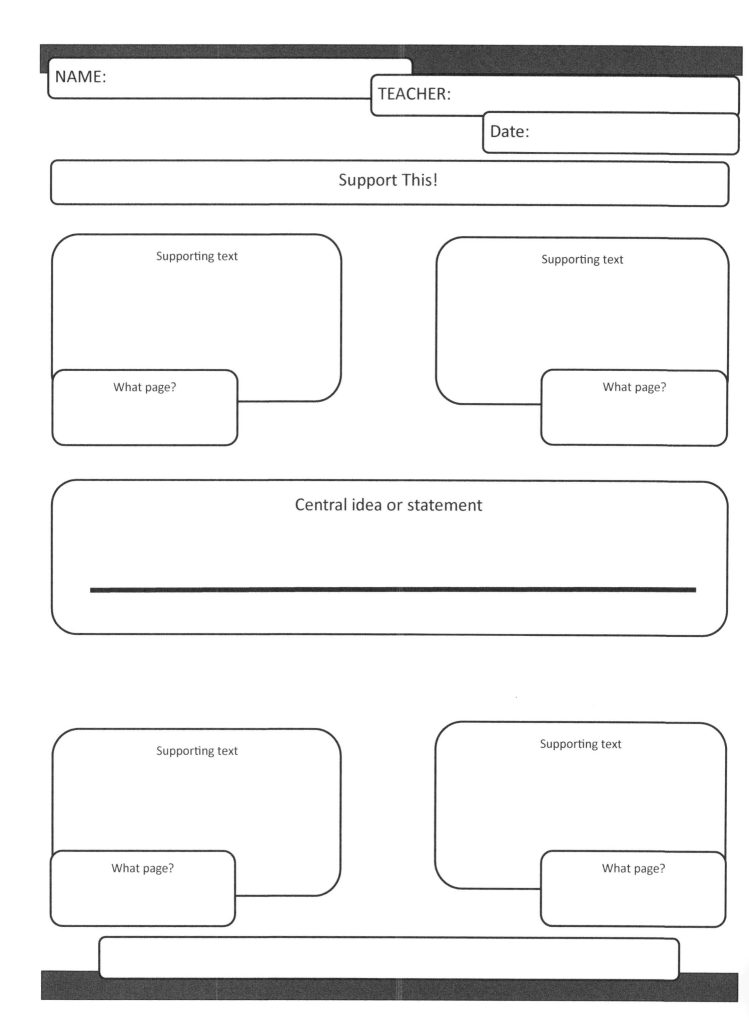

NAME:

TEACHER:

Date:

## Travel Brochure

Why should you visit?

What are you going to see?

Map

Special Events

NAME:

TEACHER:

Date:

# Top Ten List

1.
2.
3.
4.
5.
6.
7.
8.
9.
10.

NAME:

TEACHER:

Date:

## Vocabulary Box

Definition:

Draw:

**Word:**

Related words:

Use in a sentence:

Definition:

Draw:

**Word:**

Related words:

Use in a sentence:

NAME:

TEACHER:

Date:

## What would you do?

**Character:** _____

What did they do?

Example from text:

What would you do?

Why would that be better?

**Character:** _____

What did they do?

Example from text:

What would you do?

Why would that be better?

**Character:** _____

What did they do?

Example from text:

What would you do?

Why would that be better?

NAME:

TEACHER:

Date:

## Who, What, When, Where, and How

### Who

### What

### Where

### When

### How

NAME:  TEACHER:  Date:

Write a letter

To:

From:

NAME:

TEACHER:

Date:

Assignment:

NAME:

TEACHER:

Date:

## Add a Character

Who is the new character?

What reason does the new character have for being there?

Write a dialog between the new character and characters currently in the scene.

You dialog must be 6 lines or more, and can occur in the beginning, middle or end of the scene.

NAME:

TEACHER:

Date:

## Costume Design

Draw a costume for one the characters in the scene.

Why do you believe this character should have a costume like this?

NAME:

TEACHER:

Date:

## Props Needed

**Prop:**

What text from the scene supports this?

**Prop:**

What text from the scene supports this?

**Prop:**

What text from the scene supports this?

NAME:

TEACHER:

Date:

Soundtrack!

Song:

Why should this song be used?

Song:

Why should this song be used?

Song:

Why should this song be used?

NAME:

TEACHER:

Date:

## Stage Directions

List who is moving, how they are moving and use text from the dialog to determine when they move.

Who:

How:

When:

Who:

How:

When:

Who:

How:

When:

NAME:

TEACHER:

## Poetry Analysis

Date:

**Name of Poem:**

Subject:
- Text Support:

Plot:
- Text Support:

Theme:
- Text Support:

Setting:
- Text Support:

Tone:
- Text Support:

Important Words and Phrases:

Why are these words and phrases important:

Made in the USA
Monee, IL
09 March 2021